CW00525491

60

SECONDS
THAT SHAPED
THE BLUES

Written by Peter Rogers

A TWOCAN PUBLICATION

©2020. Published by twocan under licence from Ipswich Town Football Club.

ISBN: 978-1-913362-24-9

PICTURE CREDITS:
Action Images, Archant, Ipswich Town Football Club,
Mirrorpix, Press Association.

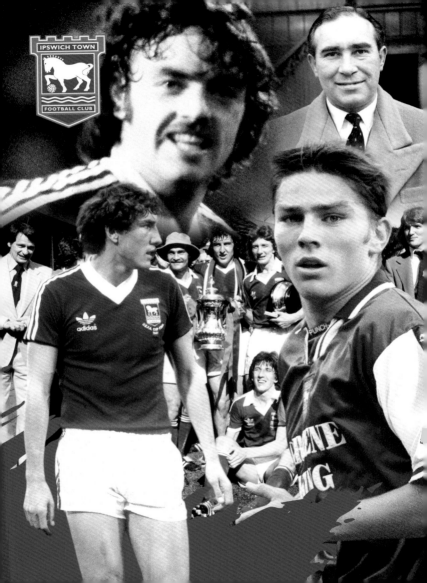

60 Seconds
that Shaped the Blues

Ipswich Town Football Club has certainly been blessed with a rich and proud history. Not only have Town provided England with their two most successful managers, but they have also sought to be a club that do things the right way - a reputation gained under the guidance of the Cobbold family who did so much for the club dating back to its formation in 1878.

League champions, FA Cup winners, conquerors of Europe and promotions aplenty, Ipswich Town has a wonderful record of success. Those past achievements have shaped the club and given supporters real pride in following the Blues' fortunes.

Narrowing over 140 years of football club history down to 60 seconds is certainly a challenge, particularly when that football club is Ipswich Town, for whom there has rarely been a dull moment!

This publication reflects on 60 key moments that have helped create the wonderful club that is Ipswich Town. A collection of games, goals, signings and managerial comings and goings, '60 Seconds that shaped the Blues' charts the ups and downs of the club both on and off the pitch.

Ask any number of Ipswich supporters to choose their favourite 60 moments from the club's past and it's unlikely you'll get two lists the same. After all, those choices come down to subjective opinion and personal preference. Hopefully these 60 entries will be acknowledged as key moments in the club's lifespan to date and will bring some fond memories flooding back.

Finally, many thanks to all associated with Ipswich Town both past and present for their contribution to the ongoing story that is Ipswich Town Football Club.

Up the Blues!

Peter Rogers

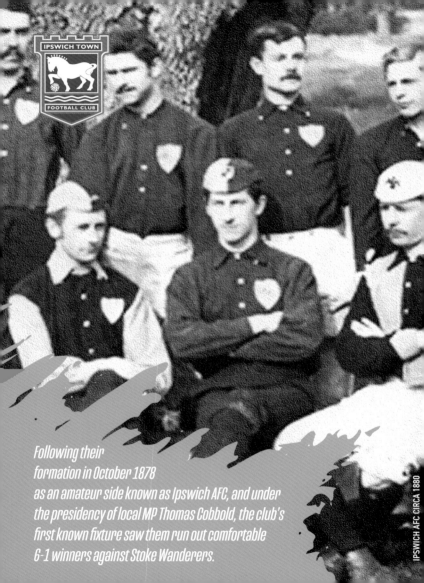

Following their
formation in October 1878
as an amateur side known as Ipswich AFC, and under
the presidency of local MP Thomas Cobbold, the club's
first known fixture saw them run out comfortable
6-1 winners against Stoke Wanderers.

IPSWICH AFC CIRCA 1880

FIXTURE:	Friendly
DATE:	2 November 1878
SCORE:	Ipswich AFC 6
	Stoke Wanderers 1
VENUE:	Broom Hill
ATTENDANCE:	Unknown

#1

Formation and First Known Match

Interest in the club soon began to grow and in 1884 they moved to Portman Road, sharing facilities with the East Suffolk Cricket Club who had been there since 1855.

The club landed its first trophy in 1886/87 after defeating a team representing Ipswich School in the final of the Suffolk Challenge Cup.

In 1888 the club merged with Ipswich Rugby Club to form Ipswich Town FC.

After invitations to join both the Southern Amateur League and the Norfolk & Suffolk League, the club joined the latter in 1899/1900. On Saturday 15 November 1902, they began their rivalry with Norwich City as the two clubs met for the very first time at Norwich's Newmarket Road home.

Once football returned after the First World War, Ipswich Town joined the Southern Amateur League and won their first of four league titles at that level in 1921/22.

1880-87

1889-90

FIXTURE:	Division Three (South)
DATE:	27 August 1938
SCORE:	Ipswich Town 4
	Southend United 2
VENUE:	Portman Road
ATTENDANCE:	19,242

#2

Town Join the Football League

Having made the decision to turn professional in 1936, Town spent two seasons in the Southern League before stepping up to join the Football League in May 1938.

GILBERT ALSOP

The club were elected to Division Three (South) at the expense of Gillingham, and would kick-off life as a member of the Football League for the 1938/39 campaign.

Under the management of Scott Duncan, Ipswich made a winning start to Football League life overcoming Southend United 4-2 at Portman Road on the opening weekend of the 1938/39 season. Bryn Davies, Gilbert Alsop and Fred Jones (2) took the mantle of scoring in Town's first League fixture.

Duncan's men made it two wins from two games, just two days later returning home from their maiden away fixture at Walsall with two points.

Town ended their debut season in the Football League with an impressive seventh-place finish in Division Three (South) having amassed 44 points with 16 wins and a dozen draws from their 42-game programme.

SCOTT DUNCAN

*Following the outbreak
of the Second World War, Town would have to wait until
1946/47 for Football League fixtures to recommence.*

MANAGER SCOTT DUNCAN (FRONT LEFT) & PLAYERS WITH THE DIVISION THREE (SOUTH) CHAMPIONSHIP SHIELD

Ipswich Town secured their first Football League title in 1953/54 when boss Scott Duncan masterminded the club's promotion to the Second Division as Third Division (South) champions.

FIXTURE: Division Three (South)

DATE: 1 May 1954

SCORE: Ipswich Town 2
Northampton Town 1

VENUE: Portman Road

ATTENDANCE: 22,136

First Football League Title

The Blues went into their final game of the season with promotion and the title secured, pipping Brighton & Hove Albion to top spot following a 2-1 victory over Newport County at Somerton Park in their previous fixture.

On an afternoon of great celebration, the result at home to Northampton Town had little consequence, but Duncan's men signed off on a winning note with their 27th league victory of the season.

Northampton took a surprise lead when Jim Feeney unfortunately put though his own net. The impressive Ted Phillips headed home the Ipswich equaliser on the stroke of half-time before then forcing Cobblers' defender Ben Collins into the game's second own-goal.

The Portman Road faithful poured onto the pitch at the final whistle to celebrate with their heroes before Town captain Tommy Parker was presented with the Third Division (South) shield.

TOMMY PARKER

FIXTURE: Division Three (South)

DATE: 20 August 1955

SCORE: Ipswich Town 0
Torquay United 2

VENUE: Portman Road

ATTENDANCE: 15,796

The Dawn of the Alf Ramsey Era

Following the team's relegation back to Division Three (South), it was all change at Portman Road during the summer of 1955.

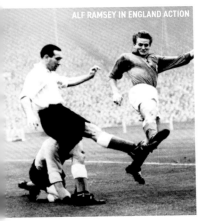
ALF RAMSEY IN ENGLAND ACTION

After just one season in the Second Division, long-serving manager Scott Duncan opted to retire having spent almost 18 years at the helm at Portman Road.

Duncan's replacement was 35-year-old former Saints and Spurs full-back Alf Ramsey. The Ipswich Board's initial plan was to appoint Ramsey as player/manager, but Alf was insistent that he would only concentrate on one job and that was to be the role of manager. On 8 August 1955 he was confirmed as Town's new boss.

Ramsey's tenure began in unremarkable fashion as Town suffered a 2-0 Third Division (South) defeat at home to Torquay United. That defeat against the Gulls certainly gave no insight as to what manager Alf Ramsey would achieve for both Ipswich Town and ultimately England.

#4

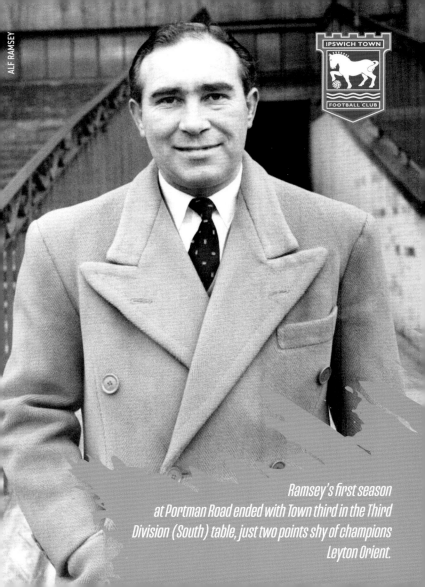

ALF RAMSEY

IPSWICH TOWN
FOOTBALL CLUB

*Ramsey's first season
at Portman Road ended with Town third in the Third
Division (South) table, just two points shy of champions
Leyton Orient.*

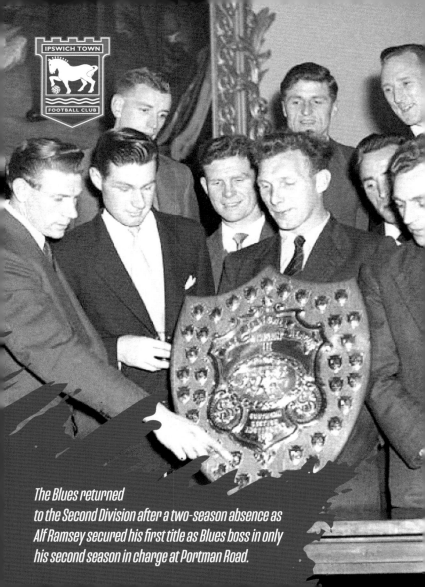

The Blues returned to the Second Division after a two-season absence as Alf Ramsey secured his first title as Blues boss in only his second season in charge at Portman Road.

FIXTURE:	Division Three (South)
DATE:	1 May 1957
SCORE:	Southampton 0
	Ipswich Town 2
VENUE:	The Dell
ATTENDANCE:	10,946

#5

Champions Again

Alf Ramsey guided Ipswich Town to the 1956/57 Third Division (South) title with a dramatic final-day victory over Southampton at the Dell.

The Blues trailed league leaders Torquay United by one point going into this final fixture on the south coast. The Gulls meanwhile were also on the road, concluding their league schedule against Crystal Palace at Selhurst Park.

With Ipswich needing to better Torquay's result, second-half goals from Jimmy Leadbetter and Basil Acres gave Town the win they needed. Meanwhile in South London, Torquay were held to a 1-1 draw. Both clubs ended the campaign with 59 points, but the Blues secured top spot thanks to a superior goal average.

The 1956/57 final Third Division (South) league table certainly made great viewing for Town fans, as not only were the Blues promoted as champions, but local rivals Norwich City propped up the entire division and were forced to apply for re-election.

BASIL ACRES

FIXTURE:	Division Two
DATE:	4 October 1958
SCORE:	Swansea Town 4
	Ipswich Town 2
VENUE:	Vetch Field
ATTENDANCE:	12,594

Crawford
Off the Mark

Centre-forward Ray Crawford joined Ipswich Town from First Division Portsmouth following a £5,000 transfer in September 1958.

Crawford marked his October debut with two goals away to Swansea. Although his brace came as Town suffered a 4-2 defeat in South Wales, Crawford's performance set the tone for a goal-laden Portman Road career.

Across his two spells with Town, Crawford's 204 league goals top the club's all-time goalscoring charts. His total Blues goal haul stands at an incredible 227 goals from 353 competitive games - a total that is unlikely to be surpassed.

Crawford's two spells with Ipswich spanned between October 1958 and September 1963. Following stints in the Black Country with both Wolverhampton Wanderers and West Bromwich Albion, he rejoined Town in March 1966 and continued to ply his trade in Suffolk for a further three years.

*Capped twice by England
during his first spell with Ipswich Town,
Ray was inducted into the club's Hall of Fame in 2007.*

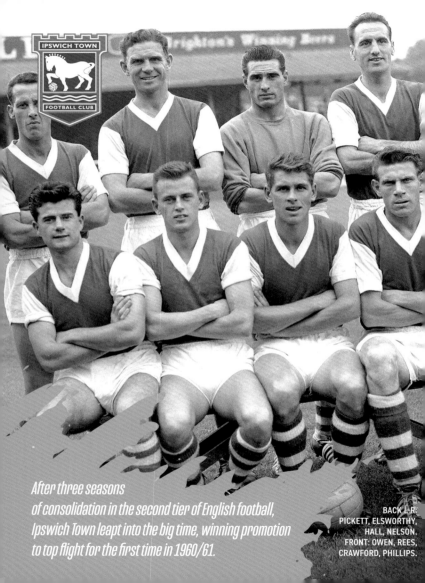

After three seasons
of consolidation in the second tier of English football,
Ipswich Town leapt into the big time, winning promotion
to top flight for the first time in 1960/61.

BACK L-R:
PICKETT, ELSWORTHY,
HALL, NELSON.
FRONT: OWEN, REES,
CRAWFORD, PHILLIPS.

FIXTURE: Division Two

DATE: 24 April 1961

SCORE: Derby County 1
Ipswich Town 4

VENUE: Baseball Ground

ATTENDANCE: 13,121

#7

Division Two Champions

Not only did Ipswich Town win promotion, but they did so in real style by landing the Second Division title and scoring a century of league goals.

Seventy of Town's ton of goals came from the strike partnership of ace marksman Ray Crawford, who netted 40, and Ted Phillips, who was on target 30 times.

In a tight two-way battle for top spot, Alf Ramsey's free-scoring side secured the Second Division title with a 4-1 win away at Derby County. Despite trailing at the break, Town simply proved too much for the Rams in the second period as a Roy Stephenson brace was followed up by goals from Ray Crawford and Dermot Curtis.

The Blues' 1960/61 title success was momentous for the club who would now face English football's First Division elite.

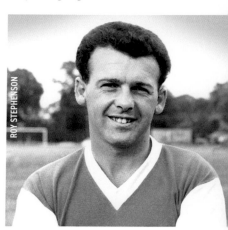

ROY STEPHENSON

FIXTURE:	Division One
DATE:	26 April 1962
SCORE:	Ipswich Town 2
	Aston Villa 0
VENUE:	Portman Road
ATTENDANCE:	28,932

The Best Team In the Land

In a historical Division One debut season, Alf Ramsey guided the First Division new boys to an incredible top-flight title success at the very first attempt.

DOUG MORAN

Locked in a two-way battle with Burnley for the title, two second-half strikes from Ray Crawford proved enough for the Blues to defeat Aston Villa 2-0 in the final game of the season.

However, Town would only land top spot if Burnley failed to beat Chelsea at Turf Moor. Shortly after the final whistle at Portman Road, news of the Clarets' 1-1 draw with Chelsea filtered though.

Ipswich Town were First Division champions!

This most remarkable of successes saw Ramsey and his players instantly earn legendary status in Suffolk. The title success also meant that Ipswich Town qualified for European football for the first time in the club's history.

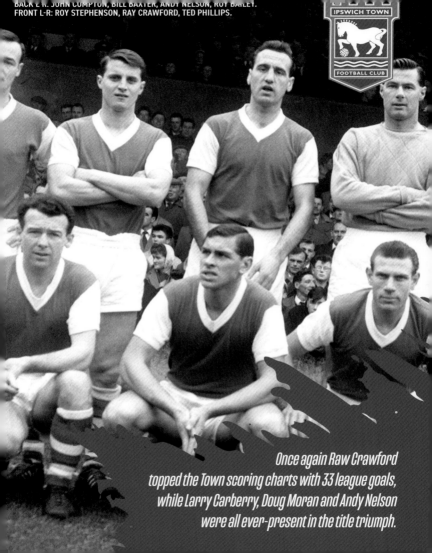

BACK L-R: JOHN COMPTON, BILL BAXTER, ANDY NELSON, ROY BAILEY.
FRONT L-R: ROY STEPHENSON, RAY CRAWFORD, TED PHILLIPS.

IPSWICH TOWN
FOOTBALL CLUB

Once again Ray Crawford topped the Town scoring charts with 33 league goals, while Larry Carberry, Doug Moran and Andy Nelson were all ever-present in the title triumph.

*Having been crowned
First Division champions the previous season,
Ipswich Town entered European competition for the
first time in 1962/63.*

FIXTURE:	European Cup preliminary round, first leg
DATE:	18 September 1962
SCORE:	Floriana 1
	Ipswich Town 4
VENUE:	Empire Stadium, Malta
ATTENDANCE:	15,784

#9

The European Adventure Begins

The Blues' faced Floriana in their European debut, a European Cup preliminary round fixture with the first leg taking place in Malta.

A recently relaid Empire Stadium pitch provided a poor surface at a ground where facilities were basic at best.

Floriana may have been top dogs in Malta, but they proved no match for Town who ran out comfortable 4-1 winners. Ray Crawford etched his name into the record books as the first Ipswich player to score in a competitive European fixture. Both Crawford and Ted Phillips scored in each half as Town took a 4-1 lead back home for the second leg.

Town thrashed the Maltese club 10-0 at Portman Road in the second leg to tee-up a first round meeting with Italian giants AC Milan.

TED PHILLIPS

FIXTURE:	Division Two
DATE:	7 May 1966
SCORE:	Ipswich Town 5 Wolves 2
VENUE:	Portman Road
ATTENDANCE:	14,201

#10

One Down
740 to Follow

Town's final home game of the 1965/66 season against Wolverhampton Wanderers witnessed legendary defender Mick Mills make his Ipswich debut.

Over a 16-year period, the full-back played a further 740 games for the club and established himself as the Ipswich Town's record appearance maker.

Mills began his marathon 741-game Town career aged just 17 and got off to a winning start after boss Bill McGarry handed him a starting place in the 5-2 Second Division victory over Wolverhampton Wanderers.

Following the arrival of Bobby Robson as manager, Mills soon struck up a close working relationship with his new boss and was named team captain in 1971. He went on to skipper the club to its greatest glories.

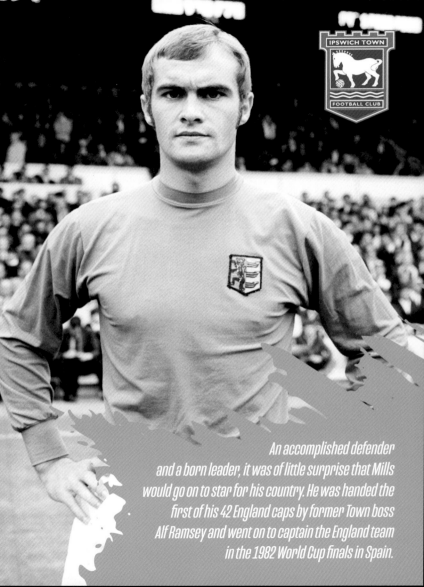

An accomplished defender and a born leader, it was of little surprise that Mills would go on to star for his country. He was handed the first of his 42 England caps by former Town boss Alf Ramsey and went on to captain the England team in the 1982 World Cup finals in Spain.

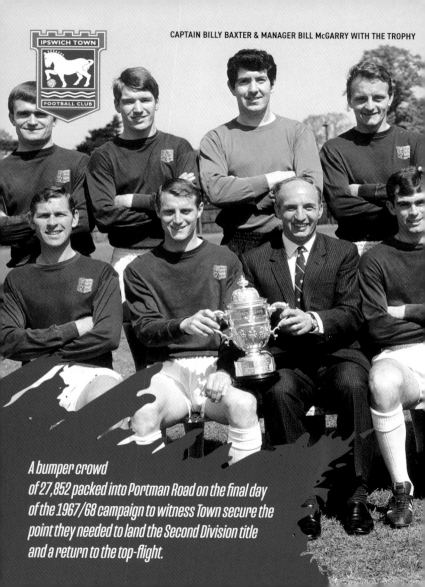

CAPTAIN BILLY BAXTER & MANAGER BILL McGARRY WITH THE TROPHY

A bumper crowd
of 27,852 packed into Portman Road on the final day
of the 1967/68 campaign to witness Town secure the
point they needed to land the Second Division title
and a return to the top-flight.

FIXTURE: Division Two

DATE: 11 May 1968

SCORE: Ipswich Town 1
Blackburn Rovers 1

VENUE: Portman Road

ATTENDANCE: 27,852

#11

Back in
The Big Time

Under the management of Bill McGarry, Ipswich went into their final fixture at home to Blackburn Rovers as league leaders and boasting a two-point cushion over both Queens Park Rangers and Blackpool.

Knowing a point would see them confirmed as champions and take the club back to Division One for the first time following relegation four years earlier, the stakes could hardly have been higher for McGarry's men.

Town continued their impressive end-of-season form and made it 15 matches without defeat as they landed the all-important point following a hard fought draw with Rovers.

Ray Crawford headed Town in front after 26 minutes before Rovers leveled the match just three minutes before the half-time break.

This title-winning success gave Town their fifth championship in 14 years, but more importantly it took the club back to the top flight.

COLIN VILJOEN

FIXTURE:	Division One
DATE:	18 January 1969
SCORE:	Everton 2
	Ipswich Town 2
VENUE:	Goodison Park
ATTENDANCE:	41,725

#12

Bobby
Robson Arrives

Following Bill McGarry's move to First Division rivals Wolves, Town appointed former Fulham boss Bobby Robson as the club's new manager on 13 January 1969.

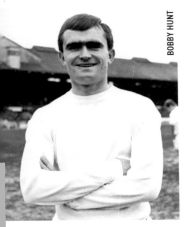

BOBBY HUNT

Robson's appointment came following Cyril Lea's stint as caretaker manager in the aftermath of McGarry's move to Molineux. Little did anyone know that when Robson first walked through the door at Portman Road, this was the man who would bring an unparalleled level of success to Ipswich and provide the club with its greatest era.

Just five days after his unveiling, Robson took charge for the first time as Town headed to Merseyside for a tough assignment against Everton. A highly eventful afternoon at Goodison Park unfolded with referee Maurice Fussey at the centre of attention. Sandy Brown gave the Toffees a 28th-minute lead before Ray Crawford levelled ten minutes later.

The match erupted seven minutes into the second half when Crawford appeared to punch the ball home for Town's second goal. Despite the home side's lengthy protests the goal stood.

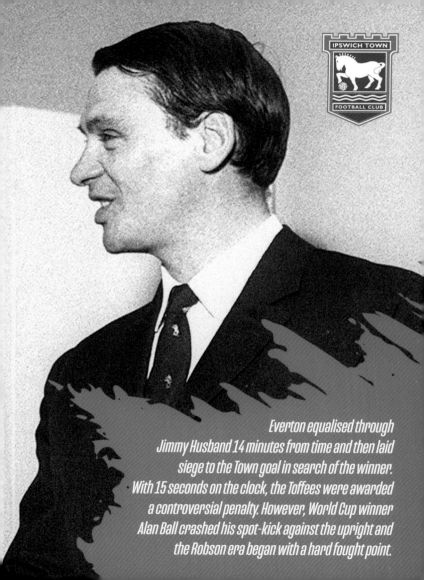

Everton equalised through Jimmy Husband 14 minutes from time and then laid siege to the Town goal in search of the winner. With 15 seconds on the clock, the Toffees were awarded a controversial penalty. However, World Cup winner Alan Ball crashed his spot-kick against the upright and the Robson era began with a hard fought point.

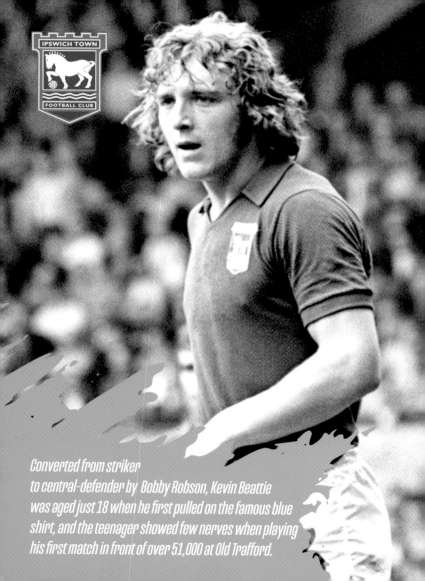

Converted from striker to central-defender by Bobby Robson, Kevin Beattie was aged just 18 when he first pulled on the famous blue shirt, and the teenager showed few nerves when playing his first match in front of over 51,000 at Old Trafford.

FIXTURE: Division One

DATE: 12 August 1972

SCORE: Manchester United 1
Ipswich Town 2

VENUE: Old Trafford

ATTENDANCE: 51,459

The Beat Begins

Robson handed youngster Kevin Beattie his first-team debut in the opening game of the 1972/73 campaign as Town ran out 2-1 winners away to Manchester United.

Beattie gave an impressive display at the heart of the Town defence, so much so that when the youngster asked United and England legend Bobby Charlton for a post-match autograph, Charlton told Beattie that his performance reminded him of Duncan Edwards and that in years to come, he would be the one signing autographs.

Only a late Denis Law goal prevented Beattie and his Town teammates from also leaving Old Trafford with a clean sheet as well as both points, after goals from Trevor Whymark and Bryan Hamilton had put them two up.

The 'Beat' went on to score his first league goal just two weeks later in a 3-3 draw away to Leeds United, and he ended his debut campaign by being named the inaugural winner of Ipswich Town's Player of the Season award.

FIXTURE:	Division One
DATE:	28 April 1973
SCORE:	Ipswich Town 1 Sheffield United 1
VENUE:	Portman Road
ATTENDANCE:	19,271

UEFA Cup Qualification

#14

Town's progress under Bobby Robson had been steady if unspectacular during his first three-and-a-half seasons at the helm - but it certainly all came good in 1972/73.

LAURIE SIVELL

After opening the season with an excellent 2-1 win over Manchester United, Town then suffered a 1-0 home defeat to arch-rivals Norwich City, as honours in the first top-flight East Anglian derby went Norwich's way. Despite that disappointment, the Blues soon dusted themselves down and produced an excellent run of form that saw them swiftly climb the First Division table.

In final home game of the season, Town secured a point against Sheffield United that ultimately proved enough to secure fourth place in the final league standings.

Trevor Whymark netted Town's final goal of the season, his eleventh in the league, as Ipswich ended a memorable campaign with their highest league finish since winning the First Division title back in 1961/62.

TREVOR WHYMARK

IPSWICH TOWN
FOOTBALL CLUB

Securing the fourth place spot in the table also resulted in Robson's men qualifying for the UEFA Cup the following season.

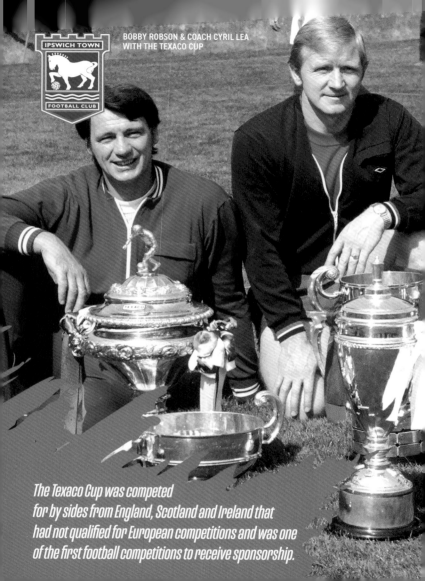

BOBBY ROBSON & COACH CYRIL LEA
WITH THE TEXACO CUP

IPSWICH TOWN
FOOTBALL CLUB

The Texaco Cup was competed
for by sides from England, Scotland and Ireland that
had not qualified for European competitions and was one
of the first football competitions to receive sponsorship.

FIXTURE: Texaco Cup final second leg

DATE: 7 May 1973

SCORE: Norwich City 1
Ipswich Town 2

Town won 4-2
on aggregate

VENUE: Carrow Road

ATTENDANCE: 36,798

#15

Texaco Cup **Winners**

Bobby Robson secured his first trophy as Ipswich boss as Town defeated local rivals Norwich City and lifted the Texaco Cup in 1972/73.

Town had defeated St Johnstone, Wolves and Newcastle United to tee-up the all East Anglian final. With the final played over two legs, Town had home advantage for the first meeting on Friday 4 May as Peter Morris netted either side of the break to help Ipswich secure a 2-1 lead to take up the A140 three days later.

In front of a Carrow Road crowd of 36,798, Ipswich once again ran out 2-1 winners to lift the trophy with a 4-2 aggregate success. There were just eight minutes on the clock when Trevor Whymark opened the scoring to put Town 1-0 up on the night and 3-1 on aggregate.

Norwich-born Clive Woods then added Town's second 13 minutes into the second half to put the matter beyond doubt, before David Cross netted a consolation strike for the Canaries with just three minutes remaining.

CLIVE WOODS

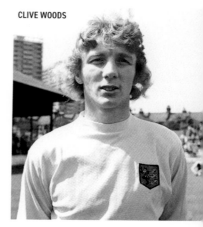

FIXTURE: UEFA CUP first round first leg

DATE: 19 September 1973

SCORE: Ipswich Town 1
Real Madrid 0

VENUE: Portman Road

ATTENDANCE: 25,280

#16

Adios
Real Madrid

Town's impressive fourth-place finish in 1972/73 saw the return of European
football to Portman Road as Bobby Robson's side entered the UEFA Cup.

MICK LAMBERT

The draw for the first round of the competition handed Ipswich the toughest of tests - Real Madrid. The Spanish giants may well be currently regarded as the most successful club side in Europe, but they were not good enough to beat an Ipswich that gave them the blues in the autumn of 1973.

Town were keen to use their first-leg home advantage to take a lead back to the Bernabeu a fortnight later. With a cracking atmosphere under the Portman Road floodlights, Town broke the deadlock early in the second half when Mick Mills' driven effort struck Madrid defender Benito Rubinan before finding its way past 'keeper Garcia Remon.

Bryan Hamilton and Mick Lambert both went close to adding a second, but it was the slenderest of advantages that Town took into the second leg.

MICK MILLS

IPSWICH TOWN
FOOTBALL CLUB

In front of 80,000
at the Bernabeu on 3 October 1973, Ipswich produced
an astute defensive display to secure a goalless draw
and an aggregate 1-0 success.

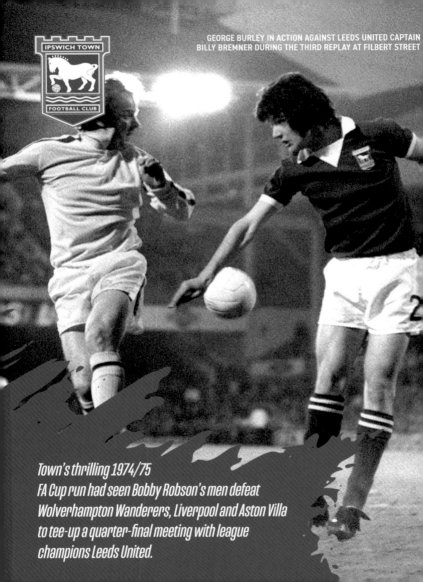

*Town's thrilling 1974/75
FA Cup run had seen Bobby Robson's men defeat
Wolverhampton Wanderers, Liverpool and Aston Villa
to tee-up a quarter-final meeting with league
champions Leeds United.*

FIXTURE: FA Cup sixth round

DATE: 8 March 1975

SCORE: Ipswich Town 0
Leeds United 0

VENUE: Portman Road

ATTENDANCE: 38,010

#17

Portman Road
Record Attendance

Despite the driving rain, it was Town who looked more likely to break the deadlock and seal a semi-final spot in front of the record Portman Road crowd of 38,010.

Striker David Johnson came closest to finding a way past David Stewart in the visitors' goal, first lifting a lobbed effort onto the crossbar and then seeing a late volley blocked on the line.

After the tie ended goalless, an Elland Road replay beckoned, but once again the two teams could not be separated. The match ended 1-1.

A second replay took place at Leicester's Filbert Street on Tuesday, 25 March 1975, but even the surroundings of a neutral venue still failed to find a winner, or a goal, as the match finished 0-0.

This marathon cup tie finally concluded at Filbert Street on Thursday, 27 March when Town won the third replay 3-2 to secure a semi-final meeting with West Ham United.

DAVID JOHNSON TAKES ON GORDON MCQUEEN

FIXTURE: FA Cup semi-final

DATE: 5 April 1975

SCORE: West Ham United 0
Ipswich Town 0

VENUE: Villa Park

ATTENDANCE: 58,000

#18

Touching
Distance of Wembley

After finally overcoming Leeds United, Ipswich Town found themselves in an FA Cup semi-final for the first time in the club's history.

Due to the prolonged nature of the quarter-final clashes with Leeds, there were just nine days between Town defeating the Yorkshire side and then facing West Ham in the semi-final.

In front of 58,000 at Villa Park, Ipswich aimed to reach Wembley for the first time. The Hammers had edged a close league encounter 1-0 when the two sides had met at Upton Park in October 1974, and another tight game unfolded in the Midlands.

After the Villa Park clash ended goalless, the two sides met again the following Wednesday at Chelsea's Stamford Bridge. In what was Town's ninth FA Cup tie of the season, this second meeting with the Hammers in the space of five days proved to be a bridge too far.

Alan Taylor put the Hammers in front before an own-goal from West Ham's Bill Jennings got Town back in the tie prior to the break. Ipswich has two further goals ruled out by referee Clive Thomas before Taylor broke Town hearts with the winner ten minutes from time.

*After dishing out
a 5-0 thrashing of East Anglian rivals Norwich City
earlier in the season, Town completed their first
top-flight double over the Canaries with a 1-0 win at
Carrow Road in April 1977.*

FIXTURE:	Division One
DATE:	9 April 1977
SCORE:	Norwich City 0
	Ipswich Town 1
VENUE:	Carrow Road
ATTENDANCE:	30,993

#19

Top-Flight Double

Although the Portman Road clash in February 1977 was something of a mismatch, the season's second meeting with the old enemy was far more evenly contested.

Trevor Whymark had been the scourge of the Canaries, netting a hat-trick in the 5-0 rout, and it was Whymark who once again proved too hot to handle the second time around.

Despite an impressive start by the home side, it was Whymark who opened the scoring after 24 minutes. Kevin Beattie headed a Brian Talbot free-kick into Whymark's path and he calmly dispatched a right-foot drive past City 'keeper Kevin Keelan.

Norwich pressed hard for an equaliser. World Cup-winner Martin Peters saw a header sail fractionally over the bar before John Ryan shaved the post with a powerful shot. The win gave Town local bragging rights, but more importantly it kept them top of the table.

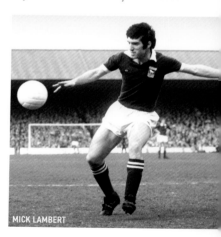

MICK LAMBERT

FIXTURE:	UEFA Cup third round first leg
DATE:	23 November 1977
SCORE:	Ipswich Town 3 Barcelona 0
VENUE:	Portman Road
ATTENDANCE:	33,663

#20

Barcelona Battered

*Having navigated their way past Landskrona Bois and Las Palmas,
Town were paired with Barcelona in the third round of the 1977/78 UEFA Cup.*

ROGER OSBORNE & JOHAN CRUYFF

Knowing a healthy lead would be needed ahead of a tricky second leg in the Nou Camp, Bobby Robson's team really turned on the style in the first meeting at Portman Road.

The Blues kept close tabs on Dutch star Johan Cruyff throughout, and took a deserved lead through Eric Gates after 16 minutes. During the second half, Ipswich really moved through the gears and doubled their lead when Trevor Whymark bundled home a loose ball after 'keeper Pedro Artola had failed to hold Paul Mariner's header.

Ipswich sent Portman Road's biggest crowd of the season into raptures when Brian Talbot headed home Town's third goal of the night 13 minutes from time.

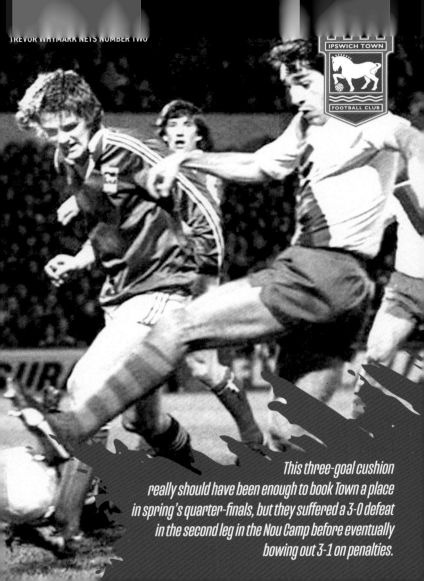

IPSWICH TOWN
FOOTBALL CLUB

This three-goal cushion really should have been enough to book Town a place in spring's quarter-finals, but they suffered a 3-0 defeat in the second leg in the Nou Camp before eventually bowing out 3-1 on penalties.

*After suffering FA Cup
semi-final replay heartache at the hands of
West Ham United in 1975, it was a case of third time lucky
for Town who defeated West Bromwich Albion to reach
their first major final.*

FIXTURE: FA Cup semi-final

DATE: 8 April 1978

SCORE: Ipswich Town 3
West Bromwich Albion 1

VENUE: Highbury

ATTENDANCE: 50,922

#21

We're Going To Wembley!

Town got off to the perfect start in this pulsating and action-packed semi-final when Brian Talbot headed home to give the Blues a 12th-minute lead.

Sadly the goal was to be Talbot's final involvement in the game. After clashing heads with Albion's John Wile when meeting Mick Mills' cross for the goal, Talbot was replaced by substitute Mick Lambert.

Town doubled their lead after 20 minutes when Mills turned from provider to scorer following a Lambert corner. With 14 minutes left, Albion were handed a lifeline when Allan Hunter fouled Cyrille Regis in the box. Tony Brown converted the penalty. Having reduced the arrears, Albion went in search of an equaliser.

With a first trip to the Twin Towers within touching distance, the tension for Town fans was verging on unbearable. Anxiety turned to excitement when John Wark met a Clive Woods cross with a thumping header to make it 3-1 and take Town to Wembley.

KEVIN BEATTIE & CLIVE WOODS

FIXTURE:	Division One
DATE:	15 April 1978
SCORE:	Everton 1
	Ipswich Town 0
VENUE:	Goodison Park
ATTENDANCE:	33,402

#22

Butch's Blues Baptism

Young central-defender Terry Butcher was handed his first-team debut by Bobby Robson for Town's trip to Goodison Park in April 1978.

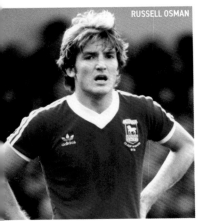

RUSSELL OSMAN

A boyhood Town fan, who had previously turned down the chance to join the youth set-up at local rivals Norwich City, Butcher would go on to establish himself as the club's top central-defender over an eight-year 351-appearance career at Portman Road.

Blessed with great aerial prowess, the ability to read the game and sense danger, Butcher also had leadership skills and bravery in abundance. He was paired alongside Russell Osman for his debut against the Toffees, and the two would form a rock-solid partnership at the heart of the Town defence for many seasons with Butcher as skipper from 1983 to 1986.

Viewed by many in the game as the best English central-defender of his generation, Butcher was capped 77 times by his country - 53 of those caps were won as a Town player.

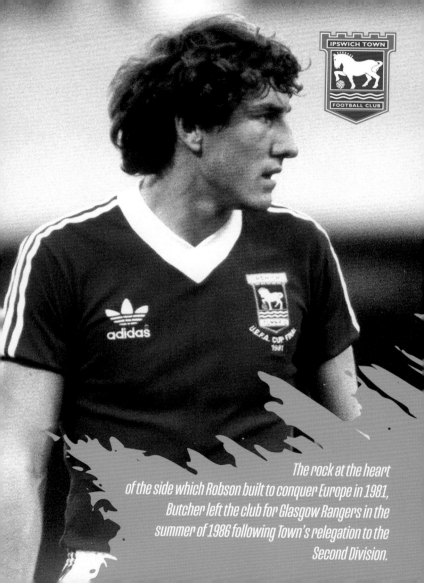

The rock at the heart of the side which Robson built to conquer Europe in 1981, Butcher left the club for Glasgow Rangers in the summer of 1986 following Town's relegation to the Second Division.

Saturday 6 May 1978
certainly goes down as one of, if not the, finest hour
in the history of Ipswich Town Football Club.

FIXTURE:	FA Cup final
DATE:	6 May 1978
SCORE:	Ipswich Town 1
	Arsenal 0
VENUE:	Wembley Stadium
ATTENDANCE:	100,000

FA Cup Winners

Fans lucky enough to secure tickets, flocked to the capital in their thousands for the club's first-ever trip to Wembley as Town faced Arsenal in the 1978 FA Cup final.

Having began the season with a 1-0 win over the Gunners at Portman Road before suffering a 1-0 defeat at Highbury in the return fixture, the final was anticipated to be another close run affair, although Town were widely recognised as underdogs. Bobby Robson's team soon made light of the underdogs tag and proceeded to dominate the game, relishing the wide open spaces that the hallowed Wembley turf offered.

After hitting the woodwork on three occasions, Town finally broke the deadlock when Suffolk-born Roger Osborne sent a left-foot shot past Pat Jennings. Amazingly, Osborne promptly fainted at the emotion of the moment. He was subsequently brought round by smelling salts before being substituted.

It proved to be a long 13 minutes for Town fans as they awaited referee's Derek Nippard's final whistle, but once it blew, unforgettable scenes of celebration followed.

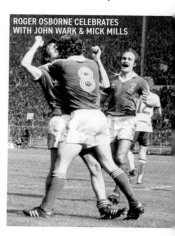

ROGER OSBORNE CELEBRATES WITH JOHN WARK & MICK MILLS

FIXTURE:	Division One
DATE:	16 September 1978
SCORE:	Wolves 1
	Ipswich Town 3
VENUE:	Molineux
ATTENDANCE:	16,049

#24

Muhren
Off the Mark

Inducted into Town's Hall of Fame in 2009, Dutch midfield maestro Arnold Muhren netted his first goal in a Town Shirt in this 3-1 away victory over Wolves.

Signed from FC Twente for £150,000 in August 1978, Muhren demonstrated an impressive array of inch-perfect passing skills in the Town midfield across four memorable seasons at Portman Road. The Dutchman possessed a wand of a left foot and developed an almost telepathic understanding with Alan Brazil, creating a host goals for the Scottish striker.

Muhren's goal came in the second half of this First Division clash at Molineux after Paul Mariner and Trevor Whymark had given Town a 2-1 half-time lead.

When later paired with fellow countryman Frans Thijssen, the duo were unquestionably the finest midfield pairing to pull on the famous blue shirt of Ipswich Town. Between 1979 and 1982 the pair produced a midfield masterclass at Portman Road.

Muhren's strike at Molineux was the first of 29 goals he netted for Town before moving on Manchester United in 1982.

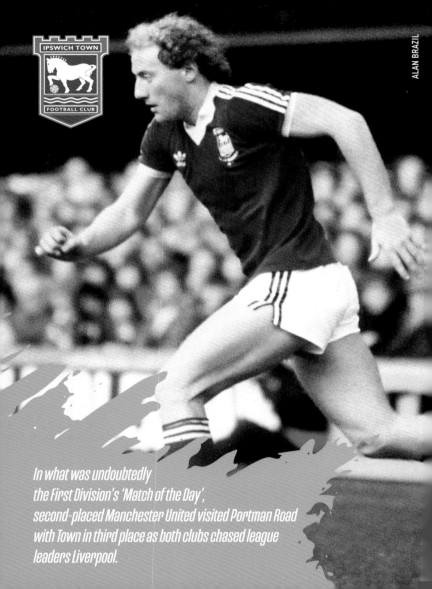

ALAN BRAZIL

In what was undoubtedly
the First Division's 'Match of the Day',
second-placed Manchester United visited Portman Road
with Town in third place as both clubs chased league
leaders Liverpool.

FIXTURE:	Division One
DATE:	1 March 1980
SCORE:	Ipswich Town 6 Manchester United 0
VENUE:	Portman Road
ATTENDANCE:	30,120

Red Devils Demolition

A close contest was predicted, but from the moment Alan Brazil beat the United offside trap to put Town in front, this match proved to be anything but close.

Brazil then turned provider, rolling the ball into Paul Mariner's path to fire a low shot inside Gary Bailey's near post for 2-0. Brimming with confidence, Bobby Robson's men made it 3-0 after 27 minutes when Eric Gates teed up Mariner for his second of the game.

More drama unfolded before the interval as United 'keeper Bailey pulled off a remarkable hat-trick of penalty saves. Bailey first denied Fans Thijssen, before Town won a second penalty, this time Kevin Beattie was thwarted before been given a second chance after the referee spotted some encroachment. Unbelievably, Bailey completed his hat-trick of heroics to keep the half-time score at 3-0.

Brazil claimed his second and Town's fourth after the break before Thijssen made amends for his spot-kick miss with Ipswich's fifth. Five minutes from time, Mariner completed the rout completing his hat-trick to a cap off an exquisite Town performance.

PAUL MARINER

FIXTURE:	First Division
DATE:	29 March 1980
SCORE:	Ipswich Town 1 Derby County 1
VENUE:	Portman Road
ATTENDANCE:	19,718

Super Cooper

Paul Cooper was already established as a penalty-saving expert at Portman Road, but in 1979/80, the Blues' stopper entered the record books in for his spot-kick heroics

March 1980 had begun with Manchester United goalkeeper Gary Bailey pulling off a hat-trick of penalty saves at Portman Road during his side's 6-0 thrashing at the hands of Town. The month ended with Cooper saving a brace of spot-kicks in Town's 1-1 draw at home to relegation-threatened Derby County.

With the score at 0-0, Cooper repelled a first-half penalty from Barry Powell at the Churchman's End before delighting the North Stand by repeating the trick after the break to deny Gerry Daly and keep the game goalless.

The outstanding Cooper was finally beaten by a Dave Swindlehurst header before Eric Gates struck the Town leveler.

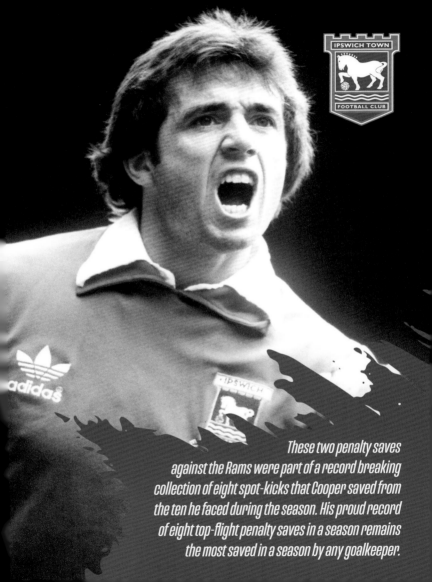

These two penalty saves against the Rams were part of a record breaking collection of eight spot-kicks that Cooper saved from the ten he faced during the season. His proud record of eight top-flight penalty saves in a season remains the most saved in a season by any goalkeeper.

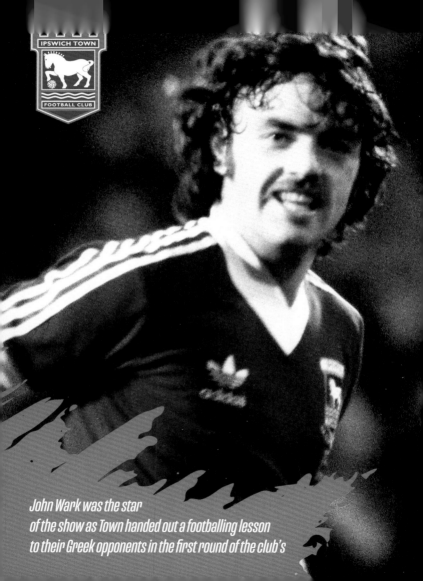

*John Wark was the star
of the show as Town handed out a footballing lesson
to their Greek opponents in the first round of the club's*

FIXTURE: UEFA Cup first round first leg

DATE: 17 September 1980

SCORE: Ipswich Town 5
Aris Salonika 1

VENUE: Portman Road

ATTENDANCE: 20,842

#27

Wark Ensures Greeks pay the Penalty

Aris Salonika provided little resistance to Town's quality, and their cynical attempts to thwart the Blues led to a busy evening for Portuguese referee Antonio Garrido.

It took Town just 13 minutes to open the scoring, John Wark converting from the penalty spot after Eric Gates had been scythed down. Two minutes later, Wark made it 2-0 when he fired home after the visiting 'keeper had failed to hold a cross from Mick Mills.

Wark completed a remarkable hat-trick inside the opening half hour when he converted his second penalty of the night, after once again, Gates was fouled in the box. George Firos was cautioned for his continued protests, and was then given his marching orders for another foul on Gates before Paul Mariner and Georgios Semertzidis had their names taken as an ill-tempered first-half came to a close.

Surprisingly, the ten men reduced the arrears early in the second half before Mariner restored Town's three-goal cushion after 61 minutes. Wark then scored his fourth and Town's fifth when he completed a hat-trick of penalties, after Gates had once again been upended.

The ill-disciplined Greek visitors were jeered off by the Portman Road crowd as Town took a four-goal cushion into the second leg.

FIXTURE: FA Cup quarter-final replay

DATE: 10 March 1981

SCORE: Ipswich Town 1
Nottingham Forest 0

VENUE: Portman Road

ATTENDANCE: 31,060

#28

Dreaming of the Double

Town maintained their exciting bid for a league and cup double in 1980/81, as they overcame Nottingham Forest in an FA Cup quarter-final replay at Portman Road.

WARK & THIJSSEN V MANCHESTER CITY

The initial tie at the City Ground four days earlier saw Town surrender a two-goal lead, but force a replay after Frans Thijssen's effort deflected in off of Viv Anderson, as the see-saw cup tie ended 3-3.

Over 31,000 fans shoe-horned themselves into Portman Road for the replay and were rewarded when Arnold Muhren's second-half strike proved enough to see off Brian Clough's men and take Town to their third FA Cup semi-final in the space of seven seasons.

The semi-final saw Bobby Robson lock horns with former Norwich boss John Bond who was now in charge of Manchester City. Villa Park was the venue for the semi-final showdown with City, but all did not got to plan.

Just as had been
the case for Town's semi-final meeting with
West Ham United in 1975, Ipswich failed to take their
scoring boots to the Midlands and suffered a
frustrating and bitterly disappointing 1-0 defeat.

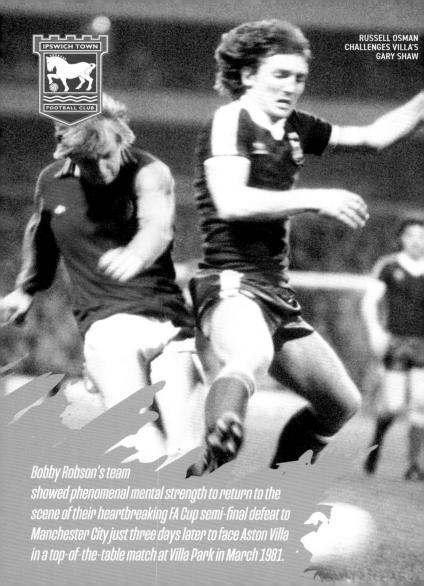

IPSWICH TOWN
FOOTBALL CLUB

RUSSELL OSMAN
CHALLENGES VILLA'S
GARY SHAW

Bobby Robson's team showed phenomenal mental strength to return to the scene of their heartbreaking FA Cup semi-final defeat to Manchester City just three days later to face Aston Villa in a top-of-the-table match at Villa Park in March 1981.

FIXTURE: Division One

DATE: 14 April 1981

SCORE: Aston Villa 1
Ipswich Town 2

VENUE: Villa Park

ATTENDANCE: 47,495

A Perfect Response

Town's league and cup double dream ended at the hands of Manchester City when a Paul Power goal settled the FA Cup semi-final meeting, but with league title glory still very much on offer, Ipswich responded in the best possible way.

Billed as the title decider in some quarters, Villa Park was packed to the rafters for Town's visit, and a truly pulsating clash unfolded. It was first blood to Town as Paul Mariner swooped on an error in the Villa defence before feeding the ball to Alan Brazil who rammed home the opening goal at the Holte End.

Brazil's goal separated the two sides at the break and Town had to withstand a barrage of Villa pressure in the second half before Mariner played in Eric Gates who hammered Town's second goal of the night past 'keeper Jimmy Rimmer.

Gary Shaw stuck a great goal to spark a grandstand finish, but Town held on to keep the title race wide open with five games to play.

ARNOLD MUHREN TACKLES DENNIS MORTIMER

FIXTURE:	UEFA Cup semi-final second leg
DATE:	22 April 1981
SCORE:	FC Cologne 0 Ipswich Town 1
VENUE:	Muengersdorfer Stadium
ATTENDANCE:	55,000

Semi-Final
Success

John Wark's goal in the first leg of this UEFA Cup semi-final meeting with FC Cologne gave Town a slender lead to take to Germany for the all-important second leg.

GOALSCORER TERRY BUTCHER

Since defeating Cologne at Portman Road, Town had seen their bid for a historic league and cup double slip from their grasp. An FA Cup semi-final defeat to Manchester City was followed by a moral boosting win over title-rivals Aston Villa, but sadly the Villa Park triumph was followed by defeats against Arsenal and bitter rivals Norwich City, leaving Aston Villa in pole position for the league title.

As Town boarded their flight to Germany, there was no hiding from the fact that all hopes of silverware were now squarely resting on UEFA Cup glory.

Ipswich went about protecting their first leg lead with a calm and sensible approach which frustrated the Germans. A solid midfield and defensive unit stood firm and on the odd occasion they were breached, 'keeper Paul Cooper came to Town's rescue.

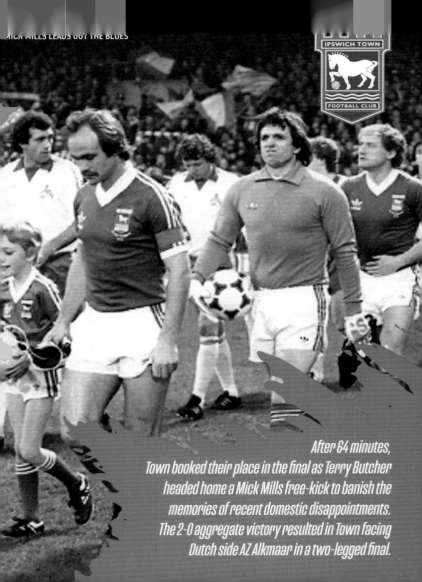

IPSWICH TOWN
FOOTBALL CLUB

After 64 minutes,
Town booked their place in the final as Terry Butcher
headed home a Mick Mills free-kick to banish the
memories of recent domestic disappointments.
The 2-0 aggregate victory resulted in Town facing
Dutch side AZ Alkmaar in a two-legged final.

ALAN BRAZIL AND ARNOLD MUHREN

A sensational display from Ipswich gave the Blues a 3-0 first leg victory over AZ Alkmaar as Bobby Robson's men really made home advantage pay in the 1981 UEFA Cup final.

FIXTURE:	UEFA Cup final first leg
DATE:	6 May 1981
SCORE:	Ipswich Town 3
	AZ Alkmaar 0
VENUE:	Portman Road
ATTENDANCE:	27,532

#31

Half Way There

AZ may have been the runaway champions of the Dutch league, but they were no match for an Ipswich side whose Portman Road display ensured they headed out to Amsterdam for the second leg with almost one hand on the trophy.

Despite a physical approach from the visitors, whose game plan appeared solely focused on preventing Ipswich rather than producing any attacking or entertaining football of their own, it was Town who opened the scoring after 27 minutes.

After Paul Mariner unleashed a powerful shot that was handled, East German referee Adolf Prokop pointed to the penalty spot and the ultra-reliable John Wark converted from twelve yards.

Town got the second half off to the best possible start as Frans Thijssen doubled the lead just 46 seconds after the re-start. With Portman Road bouncing and the visitors very much on the ropes, Ipswich scored their third goal of the night when Mariner added his name to the scoresheet.

With a fortnight to wait for the second leg in Amsterdam, Town were in fine fettle as the prize of a first European triumph heaved into view.

JOHN WARK & TERRY BUTCHER

FIXTURE: UEFA Cup final second leg

DATE: 20 May 1981

SCORE: AZ Alkmaar 4
Ipswich Town 2
Town won 5-4
on aggregate

VENUE: Stadion Amsterdam

ATTENDANCE: 28,500

#32

UEFA Cup Winners

The second leg of the 1981 UEFA Cup final certainly saw AZ Alkmaar put up a better show on home soil. However, nothing was stopping Bobby Robson's Ipswich from conquering Europe and bringing the UEFA Cup to Suffolk.

A JUBILANT BOBBY ROBSON

With a three-goal first keg lead, Town got off to the best possible of starts when Frans Thijssen volleyed home an Eric Gates corner after just three minutes.

The early strike really should have put the tie beyond doubt, but in truth, it served to trigger an Amsterdam goal-fest. The hosts levelled on the night after six minutes and then led 2-1 when Johnny Method headed past Cooper on 25 minutes. Back came Town. John Wark squared things up at 2-2, before, AZ took a deserved lead into the break when Pier Tol drove home five minutes before the interval.

Town were still two goals to the good on aggregate, but the first half had certainly given them a warning of what the Dutch side were capable of on their own patch. AZ continued to boss possession in the second half and 17 minutes from time, the final was on a knife edge as Jos Jonker converted a free-kick to shave Town's aggregate lead to one goal.

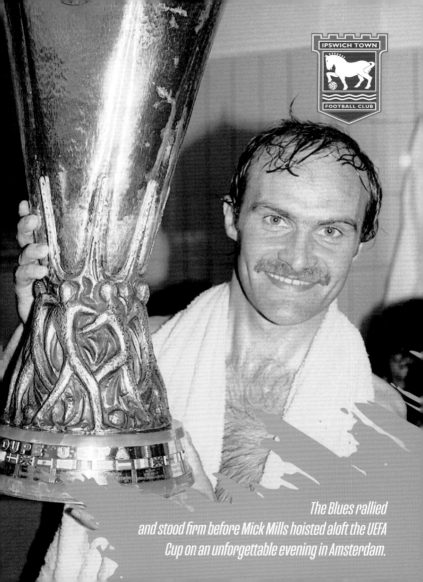

The Blues rallied and stood firm before Mick Mills hoisted aloft the UEFA Cup on an unforgettable evening in Amsterdam.

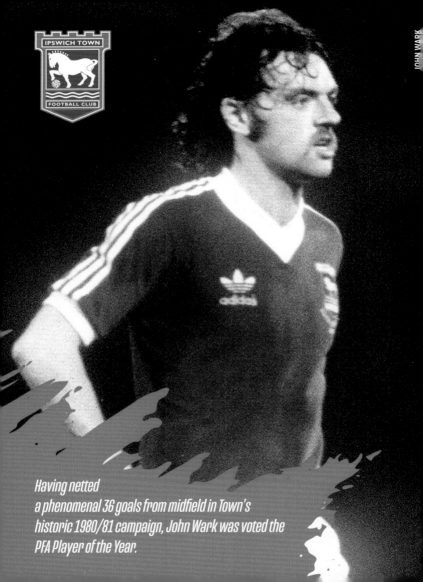

Having netted a phenomenal 36 goals from midfield in Town's historic 1980/81 campaign, John Wark was voted the PFA Player of the Year.

#33

Ipswich Players
Scoop Top Awards

Wark's outstanding contribution to Town's bid for a League and FA Cup double ended with Town winning the UEFA Cup and finishing as runners-up to Aston Villa in the First Division title race, while their Wembley dream ended at the semi-final stage.

With so many goals and match-winning performances during an unforgettable season, it was of little surprise that his fellow professionals voted Wark their Player of the Year. With Town bidding for trophies on three fronts, Wark played in an incredible 64 matches in 1980-81. Of the 36 goals he scored, a remarkable 14 came in Town's triumphant UEFA Cup run with Wark the competition's top scorer.

Such was the impression that Town had made on English football in 1980/81, Wark was not the only Blues player to be collecting an end-of-season award.

The much-coveted Football Writers Association Player of the Year title was won by Frans Thijssen, with the football journalists voting Town skipper Mick Mills as runner-up and Wark third, as Ipswich players dominated the journalists thinking.

FRANZ THIJSSEN

FIXTURE: Division One

DATE: 16 February 1982

SCORE: Ipswich Town 5
Southampton 2

VENUE: Portman Road

ATTENDANCE: 20,264

Five-Star Brazil

Striker Alan Brazil was the toast of Portman Road, the Scottish international hammering home all five Town goals when the Blues thumped Southampton 5-2.

Town had suffered a surprise FA Cup fifth-round defeat at the hands of Second Division strugglers Shrewsbury Town just three days before this First Division meeting with the Saints. However, Ipswich bounced back perfectly from their cup exit at Gay Meadow to defeat the Saints and continue their pursuit of league leaders Liverpool.

After breaking into the Town first team in January 1978, Brazil had forged a growing reputation as one of the First Division most feared frontmen and he certainly had too much for Lawrie McMenemy's Southampton on this occasion.

Brazil netted a first-half hat-trick as Town lead 3-1 at the break and continued his hot streak in the second half, beating Saints 'keeper Ivan Katalinic twice more.

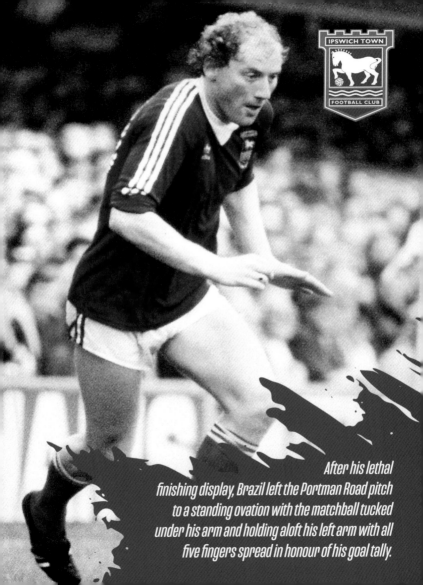

After his lethal
finishing display, Brazil left the Portman Road pitch
to a standing ovation with the matchball tucked
under his arm and holding aloft his left arm with all
five fingers spread in honour of his goal tally.

For the second time
in four seasons, Ipswich Town reached the League Cup
semi-finals. In 1981/82, Town bowed out to eventual
winners Liverpool and on this occasion arch-rivals
Norwich City stood between Bobby Ferguson's team
and a trip to Wembley.

FIXTURE:	League Cup semi-final first leg
DATE:	23 February 1985
SCORE:	Ipswich Town 1
	Norwich City 0
VENUE:	Portman Road
ATTENDANCE:	27,404

#35

Town Seal Slender Lead

With local pride and a place in a showpiece Wembley final at stake, this match certainly caught the imagination in East Anglia.

The calendar year of 1985 began with a 2-0 First Division victory over the Canaries and once again, Town made the most of home advantage, winning the first leg of this semi-final at Portman Road.

Ferguson's men got off to a flying start when Mich D'Avray headed home a George Burley free-kick after just six minutes. Town bossed the first half and created enough chances to have put the tie out of the Canaries reach before the break, let alone the second leg.

Romeo Zondervan almost added a second goal for Town late on, but saw his effort hacked off the line. Sadly, Town's inability to turn chances into goals in the first leg came back to haunt them at Carrow Road as Norwich won 2-0 en route to Wembley glory.

MICH D'AVRAY

FIXTURE:	Football League Play-Off semi-final second leg
DATE:	17 May 1987
SCORE:	Charlton Athletic 2
	Ipswich Town 1
VENUE:	Selhurst Park
ATTENDANCE:	11,234

#36

Play-Off Debut

Despite finishing fifth place in Division Two, the new Football League Play-Off system offered Town a potential return to the top flight at the first time of asking.

MICK STOCKWELL SCORES AT DERBY COUNTY

The initial Play-Off system saw the top two Second Division clubs promoted, with the third and fourth placed teams playing a semi-final over two legs while the fifth placed team faced the club fourth from bottom in the First Division in the second semi-final.

Having ended the season fifth, Town faced First Division Charlton. The first leg at Portman Road ended goalless and three days later Ipswich travelled to Selhurst Park, where Charlton were ground sharing with Crystal Palace, for the vital second leg.

Sadly, two headed goals by Jim Melrose inside the opening 20 minutes left Town's promotion dream in tatters. Steve McCall did net a consolation goal for the Blues five minutes from time, but it was Charlton who progressed to face Leeds United in the final.

Following Town's failure to win promotion, Bobby Ferguson was replaced as manager by John Duncan arriving from Chesterfield ahead of the 1987/88 campaign.

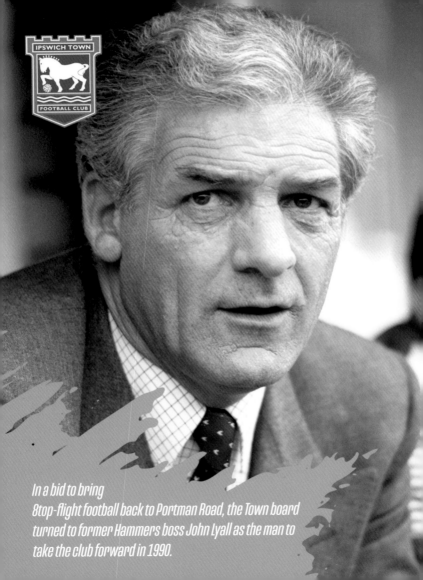

In a bid to bring
8top-flight football back to Portman Road, the Town board
turned to former Hammers boss John Lyall as the man to
take the club forward in 1990.

FIXTURE:	Pre-season friendly (Ipswich Hospital Cup)
DATE:	17 August 1990
SCORE:	Ipswich Town 1
	Norwich City 1
VENUE:	Portman Road
ATTENDANCE:	10,000

#37

John Lyall at the Helm

Lyall replaced John Duncan who in three attempts had failed to mount a promotion push during his reign as Blues boss.

A vastly experienced and well respected manager, Lyall had been in charge at the Boleyn Ground for 15 years and had twice led the Hammers to FA Cup glory. His appointment was certainly seen as a coup for Town and boosted supporters' hopes ahead of the 1990/91 campaign.

The new boss took charge of the team at Portman Road for the first time, when Town faced First Division Norwich City in a pre-season Ipswich Hospital Cup match. Lyall was given a rousing applause from the home supporters and was delighted when Ian Redford give Town a 36th minute lead.

Norwich leveled the match four minutes from time when Mark Bowen headed home, but the first impressions of an Ipswich side under Lyall's management were certainly of a positive nature.

Lyall first season in charge saw Town register another mid-table finish, but the new boss clearly had wheels in motion to deliver success the following season.

FIXTURE: Division Two

DATE: 27 March 1993

SCORE: Oxford United 1
Ipswich Town 1

VENUE: Manor Ground

ATTENDANCE: 10,525

Second Division Champions

#38

After a six-season exile from the top-flight, John Lyall's Ipswich Town returned to English football's top table as Second Division champions.

Town's timing could not have been better. This promotion-winning campaign ensured the club would compete in the inaugural Premier League season of 1992/93.

Manager Lyall promised an exciting brand of attacking football upon his appointment, and his team delivered in style. Promotion and the title were confirmed away to Oxford United when a first-half goal from Gavin Johnson in a 1-1 draw gave Town the all-important point they craved.

Town's large travelling contingent, mainly massed on the Cuckoo Lane terrace at Oxford's old Manor Ground, invaded the pitch at full-time to celebrate with their heroes as the club's six-year separation from the top flight came to an end.

Town were presented with the trophy back at Portman Road on the final day of the season when a crowd of 26,803 saw the party continue with a 3-1 win over Brighton & Hove Albion.

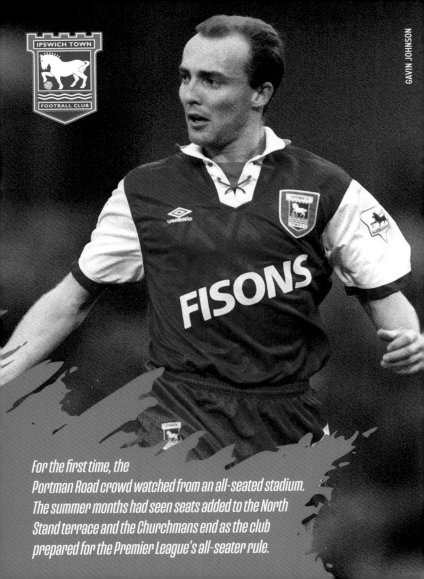

GAVIN JOHNSON

For the first time, the
Portman Road crowd watched from an all-seated stadium.
The summer months had seen seats added to the North
Stand terrace and the Churchmans end as the club
prepared for the Premier League's all-seater rule.

FIXTURE: FA Premier League

DATE: 15 August 1992

SCORE: Ipswich Town 1
Aston Villa 1

VENUE: Portman Road

ATTENDANCE: 16,818

#39

The Premier League Era

Town's first match in the newly formed FA Premier League proved to be an historic occasion at Portman Road.

Sky Sports promised fans that the Premier League would offer 'a whole new ball game', and Ipswich certainly delivered in the entertainment stakes as Gavin Johnson fired home a memorable first Premier League goal. After half an hour, the Town man picked up a misplaced pass from Villa's Steve Froggatt before blasting a thunderous 30-yard shot past Nigel Spink at the Churchmans end.

Town produced some impressive football against an expensively assembled Villa team in the first half, but the visitors took control territorially after the break as Ipswich battled to hang on for an opening-day victory.

Villa's equaliser arrived six minutes from time when Town old boy Dalian Atkinson slid home from close range. The result and performance gave all concerned with Town an optimistic feel for the season ahead.

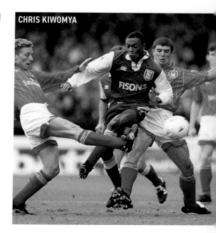

CHRIS KIWOMYA

FIXTURE:	FA Premier League
DATE:	19 April 1993
SCORE:	Ipswich Town 3
	Norwich City 1
VENUE:	Portman Road
ATTENDANCE:	21,087

#40

The Pride of East Anglia

A Jason Dozzell brace helped Town achieve a Premier League double over rivals Norwich City, and the three points that dismissed any lingering fears of relegation.

MICK STOCKWELL

The Canaries had proved the Premier League's surprise package and were involved in a season-long title bid before ending the campaign in third. However, when it came to the crunch East Anglian derby games, it was Town who came out on top in.

John Lyall's side had pulled off an excellent 2-0 pre-Christmas win over their table-topping neighbours and completed the double with this 3-1 win under the Portman Road floodlights and in front of the live Sky TV cameras.

Dozzell opened the scoring after 21 minutes, slotting home a pass from Geraint Williams and although Norwich levelled when Chris Sutton headed a 41st-minute equaliser, Town took control after the break.

The second half was just eight minutes old when Mick Stockwell restored Town's lead. Three minutes later Dozzell wrapped up the points with his second and Town's third with a low driven shot from 25 yards out.

JASON DOZZELL

FISONS

Town completed their season
with a defeat at Crystal Palace and a 2-1 home win over
relegated Nottingham Forest to end the campaign in
16th place with a 52-point return.

A true Town great,
Burley had enjoyed a 500-game playing career at
Portman Road which began with an Old Trafford debut
in 1973, before the Scot went on to make the right-back
berth his own.

FIXTURE: FA Carling Premiership

DATE: 28 December 1994

SCORE: Ipswich Town 0
Arsenal 2

VENUE: Portman Road

ATTENDANCE: 22,054

#41

Burley is Back as Boss!

With Ipswich battling against the odds to maintain their top-flight status in 1994/95, the club turned to club legend George Burley to take the club forward.

Burley was a key member of 1978 FA Cup-winning team, but sadly, injury ruled him out of Town's 1981 UEFA Cup success over AZ Alkmaar.

After representing Sunderland and Gillingham, Burley ended his playing days north of the border and cut his managerial teeth with Ayr United and Colchester United before returning to his spiritual home of Portman Road.

He first took charge of Town for a Premiership match at home to Arsenal during the 1994 festive period. Unable to prevent the drop, Burley was in charge of Town's humiliating 9-0 defeat away to Manchester United in April 1995 en route to relegation.

However, he slowly rebuilt the Town side and over an eight-year spell as boss, eventually guided the club back to both the Premier League and European competition.

FIXTURE:	FA Carling Premiership
DATE:	14 January 1995
SCORE:	Liverpool 0
	Ipswich Town 1
VENUE:	Anfield
ATTENDANCE:	32,733

Victory at Anfield

Adam Tanner was Ipswich's goalscoring hero in January 1995 on the day that the Blues finally defeated the Reds on their own turf for the first time.

CRAIG FORREST

Even in the club's halcyon days of the late '70s and early '80s, Ipswich had never been able to muster an away victory at Liverpool. However, the Anfield hoodoo was finally laid to rest on Saturday 14 January 1995, as midfielder Adam Tanner etched his name into Town folklore with a memorable first-half strike.

With Town battling to avoid the drop under new boss George Burnley, the home side were hot favourites for a routine home win and went into the game having not even conceded a goal in their previous five outings. Town were indebted to goalkeeper Craig Forrest who twice denied Rob Jones in front of the Kop during the early stages.

Town's surprise breakthrough came on 30 minutes when Steve Sedgley fed the ball to Tanner who from just inside the Reds' penalty area sent a rasping left-foot drive past David James and into the roof of the net.

In what was only his third appearance for the club, former apprentice, Tanner raced away to milk the applause of the Town fans at the Anfield Road End.

ADAM TANNER

Against all the odds,
Ipswich held on for an historic victory in George Burnley's
first away win as boss. This triumph backed up a
4-1 Portman Road success over fellow strugglers
Leicester City and gave Town hope of a great escape
in the second half of the 1994/95 campaign.

East Anglian derby matches between Ipswich Town and local rivals Norwich City have consistently delivered memorable moments of drama, delight and despair, and this was no exception

FIXTURE: Endsleigh League Division One

DATE: 14 April 1996

SCORE: Ipswich Town 2
Norwich City 1

VENUE: Portman Road

ATTENDANCE: 20,355

#43

A Huge
Slice of Luck

This much-loved local derby, at Portman Road in April 1996, provided a moment of slapstick comedy as Town had the last laugh at the Canaries' expense.

Not only were Ipswich Town seeking local pride, but also three vital points in their push for the Play-Offs. The home side opened the scoring after 23 minutes when Ian Marshall latched on to a long punt from Richard Wright before guiding the ball past Canary 'keeper Bryan Gunn.

RICHARD WRIGHT

After Jamie Cureton had equalised for Norwich just after the hour, a draw looked on the cards. However, all changed in the 86th minute when Canary left-back Robert Ullathorne played a routine back-pass to the 'keeper, only for the ball to hit a divot en route to Gunn, who subsequently totally missed his kick and allowed the ball to trickle into the empty net at the Churchmans end.

Surely the most bizarre ending to an East Anglian derby. The goal sparked wild scenes of celebration among the Town fans, and the win boosted Town's Play-Off hopes. It was also third time lucky for George Burley as he recorded his first derby win as Ipswich boss.

FIXTURE:	Nationwide Division One
DATE:	26 December 1996
SCORE:	Ipswich Town 3
	Crystal Palace 1
VENUE:	Portman Road
ATTENDANCE:	16,020

Dyer's
Debut Delight

Talented midfielder Kieron Dyer began his career with Ipswich Town and went on to enjoy Premier League fame and international recognition with England.

1997 PLAY-OFF SEMI-FINAL V SHEFFIELD UNITED

Born in Ipswich on 29 December 1978, Dyer began his career at Portman Road and swiftly progressed through the youth and reserve teams to establish himself in Town's first team. Aged 17, he debuted on Boxing Day 1996 replacing Mick Stockwell in Town's 3-1 victory over Crystal Palace.

After being handed a taste of first-team football by boss George Burley, Dyer quickly established himself one of the top young players in the country. His development soon caught the eye of many Premier League scouts who often flocked to Portman Road to keep tabs on his growing reputation.

His undoubted ability was rewarded with England caps at U21 level. Sadly, with Town remaining in the second tier, the local lad decided his future lay elsewhere, and completed a dream move to the Premier League in the summer of 1999, joining Newcastle United. Town received a then club record fee of £6M for their super-talented midfielder.

#44

In March 2011, Dyer made a romantic return to Portman Road on loan, but only played a further four games for the club while seeking first-team football and fitness. Over his two spells at Portman Road, Dyer played a total of 117 games for the club scoring twelve goals.

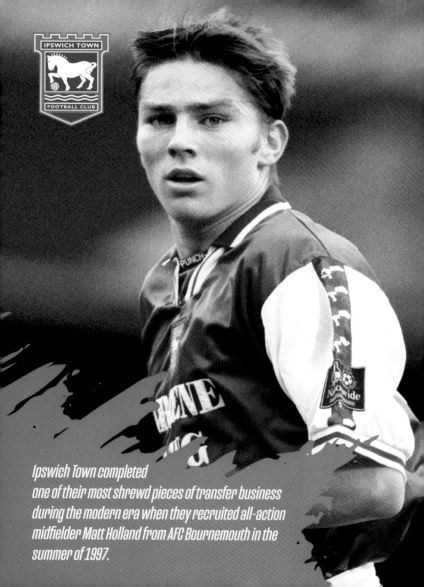

Ipswich Town completed one of their most shrewd pieces of transfer business during the modern era when they recruited all-action midfielder Matt Holland from AFC Bournemouth in the summer of 1997.

DATE: 9 August 1997

SCORE: Queens Park Rangers 0
Ipswich Town 0

VENUE: Loftus Road

ATTENDANCE: 17,614

#45

Town Swoop
For Holland

Signed by George Burley for £800,000, Holland went straight into the starting eleven as Town began their 1997/98 campaign in west London with a goalless draw at QPR.

Over the following six seasons, Holland became a firm favourite with the Portman Road faithful. His energy, commitment and consistency winning him many admirers, and the captain's armband.

Blessed with a fantastic engine and the ability to affect games at both ends of the pitch, Holland always demonstrated a desire to win the ball and get Town moving forward. An excellent scorer from midfield, he chipped in with ten goals during his debut campaign at Portman Road.

Club form won him international recognition with the Republic of Ireland, but it was his reliability that the Town fans so much admired. Remarkably, Holland missed just one league game for Town during his Portman Road career and was ever-present through his first five seasons at the club.

FIXTURE:	Nationwide Division One
DATE:	21 February 1998
SCORE:	Ipswich Town 5 Norwich City 0
VENUE:	Portman Road
ATTENDANCE:	21,858

Demolition Derby

Alex Mathie was Town's derby day hat-trick hero as George Burley's side gave the Portman Road faithful a real treat with a 5-0 thrashing of arch-rivals Norwich City.

ALEX MATHIE

With Norwich boss Mike Walker struggling to name eleven fit players, and with his out-of-sorts side without a win in their previous four games, this hammering always looked on the cards as Town continued their assent of the Nationwide First Division table.

It took Mathie just 64 seconds to begin the rout when he fired home in front of a delighted Churchmans. From that moment on, Town never looked back as Mathie wrote his name into Ipswich folklore on a wonderful afternoon for all of a blue and white persuasion.

Mathie doubled Town's lead on 27 minutes and completed his hat-trick just three minutes before the break to secure himself the matchball. He left the Portman Road pitch to a standing ovation at half-time with Town fans knowing that three precious points and local pride were already secured.

BOBBY PETTA

GREENE KING

Bobby Petta netted Town's two further goals after the break on a memorable afternoon for the home fans inside Portman Road.

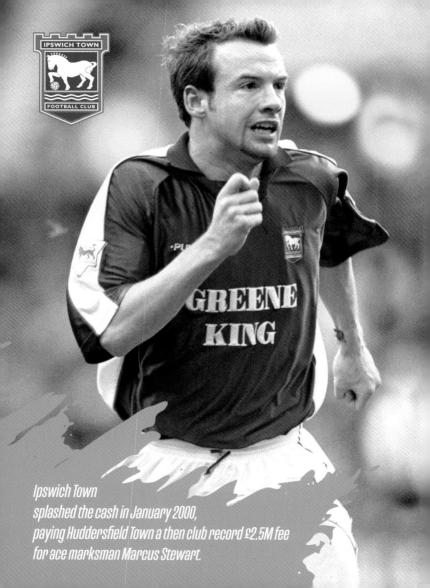

*Ipswich Town
splashed the cash in January 2000,
paying Huddersfield Town a then club record £2.5M fee
for ace marksman Marcus Stewart.*

FIXTURE:	Nationwide Division One
DATE:	5 February 2000
SCORE:	Barnsley 0
	Ipswich Town 2
VENUE:	Oakwell
ATTENDANCE:	18,287

#47

Debut Goal
For Record Signing

After three Play-Off semi-final defeats in a row, Town were determined on Premier League promotion, and the signing of Marcus Stewart was a real statement of intent.

In the simplest of terms, Stewart was signed to score the goals that would win Ipswich promotion, and the frontman certainly hit the ground running - marking his Ipswich Town debut with a goal.

Having signed from Huddersfield, Stewart made a swift return to Yorkshire for his Blues bow as Town travelled to Oakwell to take on the Tykes. Ipswich's new man was employed in a three-pronged attack alongside James Scowcroft and David Johnson. It was Scowcroft who opened the scoring after 59 minutes and just 50 seconds later, Stewart netted his first goal in Town colours to give the visitors a unassailable lead.

The bold decision to sign Stewart certainly paid off. He went on to score 27 league goals in 75 league appearances for Town, who also turned a profit when the popular striker was sold to Sunderland in the summer of 2002.

#48

Sweet Revenge
& Wembley Bound

Town finally overcame their Play-Off semi-final blues at the fifth time of asking, gaining sweet revenge on Bolton Wanderers who had defeated them in the corresponding fixture twelve months earlier.

MICHAEL JOHNSON

The two sides had drawn 2-2 at the Reebok three days earlier, so the tie was delicately poised. Bolton were swift out of the blocks and took a sixth-minute lead through Dean Holdsworth. Jim Magilton levelled from the spot after 18 minutes before Holdsworth grabbed his second to put the Trotters 2-1 ahead just before the break.

Town were awarded a second penalty on the stroke of half-time, but this time, Magilton saw his effort saved by Bolton 'keeper Jussi Jaaskelainen. Just four minutes after the re-start, Magilton made amends, scoring his and Town's second goal of the night to level the scores. Almost immediately, Allan Johnston restored Wanderers' advantage to lead 5-4 on aggregate.

The drama didn't end there. Magilton completed his hat-trick in the 90th minute, and before the final whistle blew, Bolton's Mike Whitlow received his marching orders.

Remarkably, just four minutes into extra time, referee Knight awarded Town their third penalty of the night which Jamie Clapham duly converted. Bolton's Robbie Elliott also saw red before the nine men conceded a fifth goal as Martijn Reuser struck to book Town their first trip to Wembley since 1978.

In the final club match
at the old Wembley Stadium, Town and the Tykes
produced a fitting finale for the famous old ground.

FIXTURE: Nationwide Division One Play-Off final

DATE: 29 May 2000

SCORE: Ipswich Town 4
Barnsley 2

VENUE: Wembley

ATTENDANCE: 73,427

Town Topple The Tykes

Town ended their five-year absence from the top-flight with a thrilling 4-2 Play-Off final victory over Barnsley at Wembley.

There were only six minutes on the clock when Craig Hignett's shot hit the crossbar and rebounded off Richard Wright's shoulder into the net to put the Yorkshire side ahead. Tony Mowbray headed Town's 28th-minute equaliser, but on the stroke of half time, Barnsley were awarded a penalty after Wright upended Hignett. However, the Ipswich 'keeper redeemed himself by saving Darren Barnard's spot-kick.

Town made a flying start to the second half and before the hour-mark, they had taken two huge steps to promotion - Richard Naylor put them in front on 52 minutes and when Marcus Stewart headed home a Jamie Clapham cross seven minutes later, the Town fans began to party.

The champagne was briefly put on ice when Mowbray pulled down Geoff Thomas, allowing Hignett to reduce the arrears from the spot 13 minutes from time. With the Tykes pushing hard, Town hit them on the break. Martijn Reuser broke free and raced 40 yards before smashing an unforgettable stoppage-time goal past the Barnsley keeper. Town were back up among the big boys!

MATT HOLLAND

FIXTURE: FA Carling Premiership

DATE: 19 May 2001

SCORE: Derby County 1
Ipswich Town 1

VENUE: Pride Park

ATTENDANCE: 33,239

Fabulous Fifth

Ipswich enjoyed a sensational season back in the top flight as George Burley guided Town to a fifth-place finish in the 2000-01 FA Carling Premiership.

MARTJIN REUSER

On the back of promotion, many feared a campaign of struggle back among the elite of English Football, but Town proved to be the season's surprise package.

A memorable campaign, where Marcus Stewart top-scored for the Blues with 21 goals in all competition, also saw Ipswich reach the semi-final of the League Cup.

An exceptional season concluded with Town making their first ever trip to Derby County's Pride Park. On a sunny afternoon in the East Midlands, it was the Rams who opening the scoring as Malcolm Christie latched on to a clever pass from Georgi Kinkladze before rounding Richard Wight and slipping the ball into an unguarded net.

Town levelled right at the start of the second half. Martjin Reuser's cross eventually fell to Richard Naylor whose fierce effort appeared to come off of Derby defender Haracio Carbonari on its way past 'keeper Mart Poom.

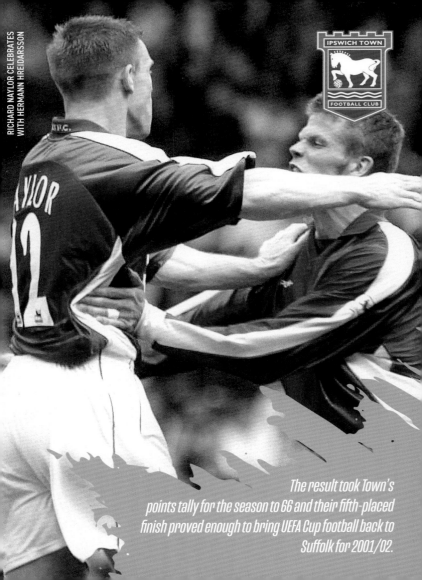

*The result took Town's
points tally for the season to 66 and their fifth-placed
finish proved enough to bring UEFA Cup football back to
Suffolk for 2001/02.*

MARCUS STEWART

*Proud winners
of the trophy 20 years earlier, Town welcomed Torpedo
Moscow to Portman Road for opening game of their
2001/02 UEFA Cup campaign. After a rare Titus Bramble
goal ensured the first leg ended 1-1, Ipswich were left
with a tricky trip to the Russian capital to negotiate
seven days later.*

FIXTURE: UEFA Cup first round second leg

DATE: 27 September 2001

SCORE: Torpedo Moscow 1
Ipswich Town 2
Town won 3-2
on aggregate

VENUE: Luzhniki Stadium

ATTENDANCE: 10,000

#51

Memorable
Moscow Victory

Despite home advantage, Torpedo operated with a defensive mindset and appeared happy to defend their precious away goal and settle for a goalless draw.

Against stubborn resistance, George Burnley's men found scoring opportunities hard to come by during the opening 45 minutes. It was the home side playing on the break that had the better chances. However, Town broke the deadlock just a minute into the second half to take control of the tie. After a Mark Venus corner wasn't cleared, the ball fell to Finidi George some six yards out, who fired home a priceless away goal.

FINIDI GEORGE

Just eight minutes later, Town put themselves firmly in the driving seat for a place in the second round draw. Marcus Stewart doubling their lead from the penalty spot after George had been held back.

Torpedo pulled a goal back after 65 minutes through Dmitry Vyasmikin and Town were grateful to their record signing Matteo Sereni in goal who pulled off two great saves as the Tractor Boys progressed, winning the tie 3-2 on aggregate.

FIXTURE: UEFA Cup third round first leg

DATE: 22 November 2001

SCORE: Ipswich Town 1
Inter Milan 0

VENUE: Portman Road

ATTENDANCE: 24,569

Alun Sinks
Inter Milan

After overcoming Helsingborg IF in the second round, Italian giants Inter Milan provided Town's next UEFA opposition in an eagerly-awaited third round tie.

With star-studded opposition, including Toldo, Zanetti, Seedorf and Ventola, the match attracted interest on a national scale and was broadcast live on the BBC Two.

Despite struggling for domestic form, George Burley once again managed to get his side firing on all cylinders in Europe. Town appeared to use the underdogs tag to their advantage, and with expectation and pressure removed, they produced an almost fearless performance on another memorable European night at Portman Road.

An impressive first-half performance saw Town more than hold their own against top quality opposition and in the second half they made the breakthrough to take a slender lead to the San Siro a fortnight later. Alun Armstrong was the hero of the hour as he headed home a delightful Jamie Clapham cross nine minutes from time.

Town held out for an historic home win, but sadly Inter Milan proved far too strong in the second leg, winning 4-1 and progressing into round four.

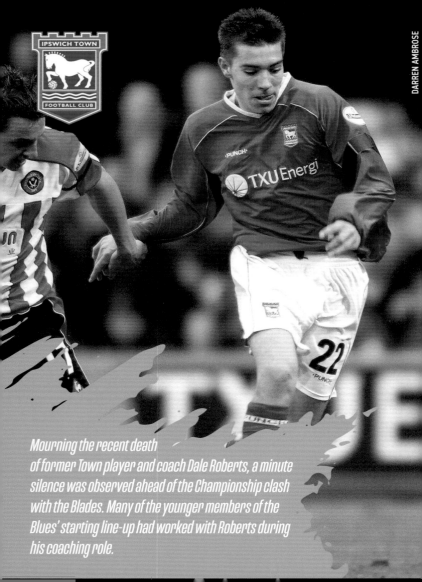

Mourning the recent death of former Town player and coach Dale Roberts, a minute silence was observed ahead of the Championship clash with the Blades. Many of the younger members of the Blues' starting line-up had worked with Roberts during his coaching role.

FIXTURE:	Nationwide League Division One
DATE:	8 February 2003
SCORE:	Ipswich Town 3 Sheffield United 2
VENUE:	Portman Road
ATTENDANCE:	26,161

#53

The Darrens Doing It For Dale

It was two of the club's homegrown heroes, Darren Bent and Darren Ambrose, who helped inspire a great comeback on an emotional afternoon at Portman Road.

Now under the management of Joe Royle, Town endured an awful first half. Ipswich were reduced to ten men after 20 minutes when Pablo Counago saw red for violent conduct following an off-the-ball clash with Blades' midfielder Michael Brown.

The ten men were punished further when Peter Ndlovu opened the scoring for the visitors as the half drew to a close and when Dean Windass doubled the Blades' lead within five minutes of the restart, the outcome was certainly looking bleak from a Town perspective.

Royle's men were given a lifeline when Bent volleyed home his 12th goal of the season after 57 minutes, and the striker turned provider in the 78th minute when he crossed for Ambrose to head past United goalkeeper Paddy Kenny for the equaliser.

Town completed a memorable turnaround in fitting memory of Dale Roberts when Ambrose crossed for Bent to grab his second goal of the game two minutes from time.

DARREN BENT

FIXTURE:	Coca-Cola Championship
DATE:	5 February 2006
SCORE:	Norwich City 1
	Ipswich Town 2
VENUE:	Carrow Road
ATTENDANCE:	25,402

The Hand Of Haynes

After suffering three back-to-back East Anglian derby defeats, Ipswich restored local pride as Danny Haynes created his 'Canary Crusher' reputation.

LATE WINNER CELEBRATIONS

Norwich handed debuts to Robert Earnshaw, a £2.75M signing from WBA, plus loan recruits Jonatan Johansson and Zesh Rehman from Charlton Athletic and Fulham respectively. However, the new signings and the remainder of Nigel Worthington's expensively assembled side were no match for a bright and vibrant young Ipswich side who thoroughly deserved the local bragging rights.

Despite Johansson giving Norwich a 33rd-minute lead when he latched on to a Youssef Safri through ball, before lifting the ball over Lewis Price, Town had been the better side during the opening exchanges.

Joe Royle's men were not behind for long and levelled five minutes later when Jimmy Juan's free-kick took a deflection off the Norwich wall on its way past Robert Green. It appeared the two old foes would take a point apiece until Town forced a late winner in controversial circumstances.

DANNY HAYNES

*Matt Richards' cross
was met by the head of Alan Lee and the ball fell to
Haynes who bundled the ball home with his arm.
Luckily for Town the match officials awarded the goal
which was just reward for a Town team who
deserved to be derby winners.*

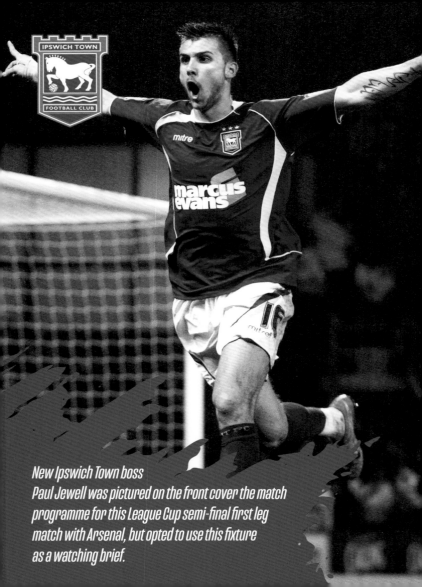

New Ipswich Town boss
Paul Jewell was pictured on the front cover the match
programme for this League Cup semi-final first leg
match with Arsenal, but opted to use this fixture
as a watching brief.

FIXTURE: League Cup semi-final first leg

DATE: 12 January 2011

SCORE: Ipswich Town 1
Arsenal 0

VENUE: Portman Road

ATTENDANCE: 29,146

#55

Priskin is the Jewel in the Crown

Ian MacParland remained in charge following Roy Keane's exit, while Jewell enjoyed a warm reception from the full house before taking his seat in the Directors Box.

Clearly inspired by their new manager watching on, Ipswich produced an excellent performance against Arsenal just three days after beginning the post-Keane era with a 7-0 FA Cup mauling at Chelsea.

This win came courtesy of a second-half Tamas Priskin goal and left Town on the brink of their first appearance in a Wembley Cup final since 1978. For those who like their omens, Priskin's goal also came in the 78th minute. With a new manager unveiled and a victory over a top Premier League outfit, this was a memorable night for all concerned at Portman Road.

Sadly despite the euphoria of this win there was still the second leg to navigate at the Emirates Stadium later in the month - a game in which the Gunners ran out comfortable 3-0 winners to seal their place in the 2011 League Cup final.

PAUL JEWELL

FIXTURE: NPower Championship

DATE: 15 February 2011

SCORE: Doncaster Rovers 0
Ipswich Town 6

VENUE: Keepmoat Stadium

ATTENDANCE: 8,448

#56

Hat-Trick Hero

The reputation of 17-year-old Town forward Connor Wickham continued to grow after the academy graduate netted his first professional hat-trick.

Ever since becoming the club's youngest ever player when he debuted against Doncaster Rovers in April 2009, aged just 16 years and eleven days, there had been a steady flow of Premier League scouts monitoring his progress.

Wickham and his Ipswich teammates certainly turned on the style when they hit Doncaster Rovers for six two years later.

Paul Jewell's Blues gave their hosts a real footballing lesson as they cruised into a 3-0 half-time lead, before eventually winning this Championship fixture 6-0. Wickham netted his first goal of the evening to make it 3-0 on 42 minutes, after a Sam Hird own-goal and a Colin Healy strike had seen Town take a 2-0 lead.

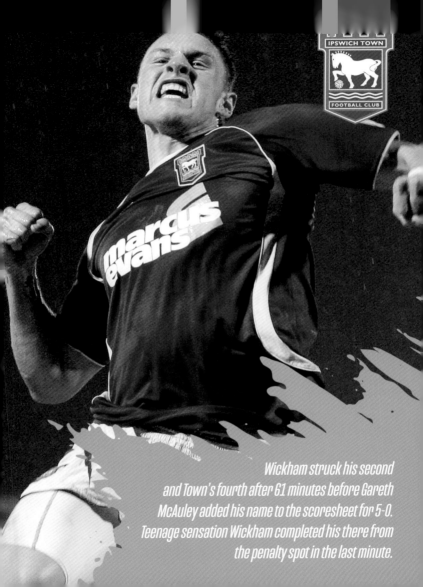

Wickham struck his second and Town's fourth after 61 minutes before Gareth McAuley added his name to the scoresheet for 5-0. Teenage sensation Wickham completed his there from the penalty spot in the last minute.

Routed to the foot of the Championship table and staring down the barrel of League One, Ipswich Town sent out an SOS to experienced former Republic of Ireland manager Mick McCarthy to succeed Paul Jewell.

FIXTURE: NPower Championship

DATE: 3 November 2012

SCORE: Birmingham City 0
Ipswich Town 1

VENUE: St Andrews

ATTENDANCE: 18,063

Mick to the Rescue

On a weekend when four new managers were unveiled in the Championship, it was McCarthy's appointment that arguably carried the greatest weight.

McCarthy sent his new troops back to basics, with a 4-4-2 formation chosen for his opening game away to Birmingham City. The new manager got off to the best possible start as Town won their first league game in twelve.

On-loan striker DJ Campbell netted his third goal in an Blues shirt having been set up by Lee Martin after just eight minutes. Town then produced a resolute defensive display to record this vital win which proved the first step on the road to Championship survival. Over the coming months McCarthy guided Ipswich Town to a 14th-place finish with a 60-point haul.

Mick McCarthy's appointment proved to be one of owner Marcus Evans' shrewdest moves, as the well-respected boss provided stability and progress at Portman Road before mounting a serious promotion push in 2014/15.

FIXTURE: Sky Bet Championship Play-Off semi-final first leg

DATE: 9 May 2015

SCORE: Ipswich Town 1
Norwich City 1

VENUE: Portman Road

ATTENDANCE: 29,166

#58

Promotion Bid

Ten seasons on from the club's last Play-Off campaign, Town qualified for the Championship Play-Offs again following an excellent 2014/15 campaign.

Such was Town's impressive form under the astute management of Mick McCarthy, they were in the automatic promotion picture at the turn of the year. With 27-goal Daryl Murphy leading the line, the Blues recorded many memorable victories, including the 4-1 rout of Leeds United at Portman Road and a 4-2 triumph at Brentford on Boxing Day. The regulation season ended with Town securing the final Play-Off spot and a semi-final showdown with arch-rivals Norwich City.

In what was billed as the biggest East Anglian derby of all-time, the first leg was scheduled for Portman Road. A packed house welcomed the two sides on to the pitch in an electric atmosphere and saw Town enjoy an impressive start to proceedings.

Although Norwich took a 40th-minute lead through Jonny Howson, Town struck back before the break when Paul Anderson's equaliser almost rocked Portman Road to its foundations such was the roar of delight that greeted the winger's goal at the Churchmans End.

Despite suffering a 3-1 defeat in the second leg, Anderson's goal in that first meeting remains a great moment for the younger generation of Town fans.

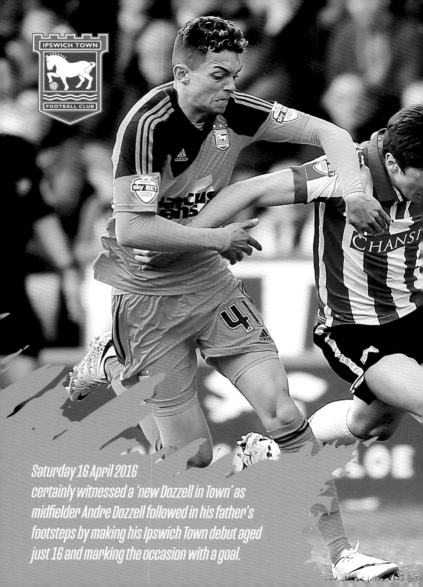

*Saturday 16 April 2016
certainly witnessed a 'new Dozzell in Town' as
midfielder Andre Dozzell followed in his father's
footsteps by making his Ipswich Town debut aged
just 16 and marking the occasion with a goal.*

FIXTURE: Sky Bet Championship

DATE: 16 April 2016

SCORE: Sheffield Wednesday 1
Ipswich Town 1

VENUE: Hillsborough

ATTENDANCE: 25,082

#59

There's a New Dozzell in Town

Andre is the son of former Town midfielder Jason, who played over 400 games for the club across two spells at Portman Road during the 1980s and '90s.

Andre replaced Kevin Foley during the half-time interval of Town's Championship match away to Sheffield Wednesday. With the Blues trailing to a Fernando Forestieri goal, Dozzell Junior stepped up to score Ipswich Town's 71st-minute equaliser to seal a point from a tough 1-1 draw against the promotion-chasing Owls.

An exciting young talent with pace, excellent close control and a real eye for a pass, Dozzell's talents have been recognised by England at youth level and the attacking midfielder certainly appears to have a great career ahead of him.

However, the local lad with such strong links to past glories at Portman Road will never forget his goalscoring debut for the Tractor Boys.

JASON DOZZELL

FIXTURE:	Sky Bet Championship
DATE:	6 May 2018
SCORE:	Ipswich Town 2
	Middlesbrough 2
VENUE:	Portman Road
ATTENDANCE:	18,829

Bart's
Hat-Trick

Popular Polish goalkeeper Bartosz Bialkowski completed a hat-trick of back-to-back Player of the Season awards as Town ended 2017/18 with a 2-2 home draw with Boro.

Although John Wark has won the award on four occasions, only Bialkowski was been presented with the award in three consecutive seasons.

The 6ft 4in stopper joined Town on an initial two-year deal in the summer of 2014 from Notts County and played a starring role as Mick McCarthy's men reached the end-of-season Play-Offs.

He was first named Player of the Season in 2015/16 as Town ended their season seventh in the Championship. Supporters then voted him their top performer once again twelve months later and his hat-trick was completed when he received the Harwich Rosebowl yet again in 2018.

An excellent shot-stopper who always gave real confidence to those playing in front of him, Bialkowski made 178 appearances for Town. Following the club's relegation to League One in 2019, the Pole moved to Millwall on loan before completing a permanent move to South London.

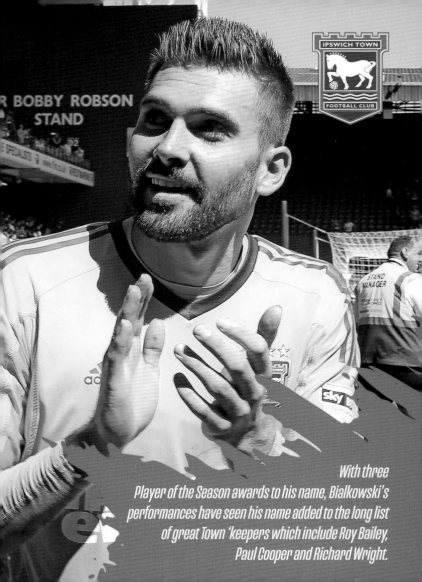

With three Player of the Season awards to his name, Bialkowski's performances have seen his name added to the long list of great Town 'keepers which include Roy Bailey, Paul Cooper and Richard Wright.

Up the Blues!